GW01017928

Antifreeze
Keston Sutherland

Some of these poems have appeared previously in the following magazines: *CCCP*, *The Gig*, *Jacket*, *Masthead*, *Parataxis*, *QUID*; and in the anti-Bush anthology *100 Days* (Cambridge: Barque, 2001) and *New Tonal Language* (London: Reality Street, 1999). My thanks to their editors for support and encouragement. *Mincemeat Seesaw and [Bar Zero]* were published as pamphlets by Barque in 1999 and 2000 respectively. The poem 'As life were or were not' first appeared in *Hate's Clitoris and Other Poems*, published by Barque in 1997. Essays by Keston Sutherland on poetry, philosophy and Capitalism can be seen online in *Jacket* magazine and on paper in *QUID*.

published by Barque Press
c/o A Brady & K Sutherland
Gonville and Caius College
Cambridge CB2 1TA
United Kingdom

http://www.barquepress.com

First published 2002

British Library Cataloguing-in-Publication Data
A catalogue record for this book is available from the British Library

isbn 1-903488-25-7 paperback

to Andrea

Content

TEN PAST NINE

In my speech shines a radiant energy,
I can destroy hype, the wind flashes with its end,
fury and barriers become smashed
                    out, the music chars hype
broke out from me. I sing and the serrated horizon
tilts, dirt splashes become zero each. We are
okay. I am not even a fucking person any more.
                    Without the bloom
of flowers set to crash, and without day after day,
antique throats would char. I am not even
despite fire victimized but am okay. The

grainy void over my speech flares and yellows,
day after day remains, ashen, vital. The things I
do say distort hype, which may become over,
                    destroyed that
is to say our worst speech. A face at
my window faces that. Without extrapolation
on me what could become smashed,
                    you cut
deep into her tongue with broken glass,
with your fist you strike out. I am ready
today, I can reduce the significance of love.

THE LITTLE MATCH GIRL

Shows you up higher the imperiled second
outbreak in misery how we each can destroy
that they said, by perilous star
flipped out across an outbracketed sky,
            by the adamant wayside,
where in tolerated adroit opposition
they said we stand or fall, the wall can become
transparent like gauze,
stops there and readies herself for conflict
            resolution it says
you picked that formalized modes of
arbitration, formalized modes of erotic happiness,
the star bangs you think highly
across or sideways can an adduced fire thread
            they ask you
to envyless sedition, as the preferable
sun budges out, can it thread you to distort out
you're breaking up try no try okay
thread you to the panic of indefectible
            vanity, as in love the skyslide
impossible you are they
say, lights were shining from all
the windows and the dark
brown leaves in the hearth
            catarrhal screw up and flash.

In the brief glow, imaginative corruption to near
zero visibility of the proletariat
wednesday I came to my senses they said no
to her, contributing by impractical echo
            to rapid and shallow
breath urgent dyspnœa send the thuds in good
you see an impersonated face
elicit combustion of the origin of mediated
expression boy took her right slipper
            profuse hectic sweats,
nothing to eat in the house but consolidated relish,

she wanted to keep herself warm, they said
and very far from inert the stricken
fence hinted at convenient distress and downfall
            raked through blood
saw teeth there, I saw a complete hand made
me wait and scared, trash cozens
dingo budgie flares up fuck you shut up it,
friends enter the room
            used was milk of sulphur
they said lights were shining from all
the windows, the dark then became reduced,
for them thought of highly,
once this fastened see the imperiled star,
            diremption of industrial and political

conflict. See the shadow of remorse,
preened, tremulous and frigid
tiny feet are stretching there, a match beside
them tinkles baghdady, the patient
            feels this glow of heat run
away through both sides of chest,
the affinity in 1914 of hydrogen and precipitated
sulphur, they were so big they
from my feet, destroyed by cartwheels,
            can this be the day
light crapped over a grille town say no
they said they were communicated barricaded
faces they town moved into
long streaks of fire across an incorruptible sky
            this violence has
declined, and has been replaced by formalized
modes of arbitration, you are
among them, the modes reach out for you
in unutterable love they reach out for
            you please take them
scratches a divisible face, they are said
here, from the apices of both lungs
brilliantly consumed and without this vanity of
any kind smashes that, may she out
            spoken for now, just say yes.

9

SLITS IN THREES ODE

1

You mitigate the fever of the scrub, truck, bulletin
faraway idiot, you as teeth comb
gashes through preserves, make finalized light

stroke of cracked, of feed puerile
damage to you no end overmuch visible carry
out days achieve fact to fact be there,

be polemical, issue the wind decree,
floats through eternal stop you are bind
are crash of the exchange, feasible tang and shut

gray out, jump about the room
picking an exact slot forever go in treacly
has you by a liberated throat.

2

Only you mess up the oil scare, lonely
tags a face envisages and default beet, tonic
universe fiasco, the wind cut

feasibly into strips do an outlook
do always committed to blank and amorous
where the gray shone, are help

them not to die fish
parcels littered bounce up a star queasy
squashed and ground in decide you

could prepare a change round
mouthful of amateur maggot honey for
now okay scrap you, rubrics at dawn.

3

As an abated scruple whose perhaps you
saw it derange a valid rainbow,
whose descry quickly be a love format take

you saw them face explode it
rained night and to morning jump over
the sky that flip crease

ever since the day collides whose finished
type of visibility airs are
screw the wind down, do exact cancel out,

bandage the hurt water, thereupon
cannot bitch too prosperously
make you reluctant wipe that grin off.

4

Stretch only to that famish divert
everything it is you must possibly accept,
bollocks to the flame strawberry

rots out panic finesses the Chávez article
bus depot, clippers,
what a face either way be a squeeze in

into the chivalrous rigmarole of validity,
into the pristine offshoot you
is that the time, do cryptonormative

flinches you bargained for, do
the stars remain alert and well travestied
ratio of dysgenic oyster to Islam.

5

What the trick is to produce a scintillant,
beneath cloud cover allegorizing mission time,
onto whose knees or in fleshy

spate of you be that rudder in cop boreas,
loosing avert loosing strip
them of pain and agitated counterreckon do

key errors to recall three of which
am not yet blind, pushed too
rapidly for heavy industry two retained

government structures of the colonial era,
three, failed to predict sharp
rise in interest, sink out in a depicts flash.

6

Mutilated hourly false control, verified
chip away verges cast out
verges to remain however free, past

the streetlight courses upon arcades runs
alerts the client backdoor shot
like a bolt through were you vivid on

cue drub expiry and incipience, they are clearly
no match for a mute disquiet,
nor for the scar spangled rescind guy pass

sentences on fire, you then borrowed the trowel,
and so throw up an assuaging sea
of ways to make a breathless living.

7

Vanish you life incorrupt, specializes in makes
of which like often or lately,
emending the tree packet, scoops net out

brought to fastidious outrage monkey shit
the shower rips up you hand,
very much want to become impassible

Oh! nicht einmal die Gnade, mit dir
freight lolls about you loll about
panic in the future rivet, a stream thorny go

into awaiting deals and pass fire,
bits of that vacate are solemn their nozzle out
shines burnish it, gag you are live act.

A LOVE SONG

As never the day collapses throw
        instead your face down,
fashion a blind the brevity of
        you may diminish, the USAF drops

away and far too much I
        ravenously vex nothing except you,
shook your head and flashes
        drop or a grated star

you had me manic with happiness
        in us dissevered,
from the spit of a longwinded sky
        and elsewhere its summary

flashes also cut a blind
        down and the trimming scapelark
you see drops, you alone
        see, and so do we love together.

A BANG COVERS ME

You were through the rectangular slot down
partway to the side where the echo fit
not envision you. I could do with that. You
          pay what for
now may attention, were thrown against
people all flashing and melting. Does
that hurt. Does it matter now too, hyped too
          shut up about
were paralyzed. The division of separate
face it you can fuck me anytime, are
you how late you are, please, stop. Indirect

blast injuries chiefly due to roof destroy,
by crushing and trapping head. Some
place beneath there, through so the dreamy
          prevents you
cannot see where you are. Shout out your
forget. Does the situated light can,
secondary to the devastating blazes over
          look in my eyes,
patch up the broken glass, at ease they
do not ask who seizes them. You can
want to do it here. Make up your mind.

LOSS OF LIFE

It's loss of life not to be yours cringes the ripped tin,
    inert it remonstrates feel battered, become long
        since passed echoes the sandwich-paste too
and flight to the repaired wish cancer settling
    up striking the bill, washing the out-screened
        promises she'll not make lightly arranged
to say that: assume you drive a total of thirty-six
    miles to and from work each day
        and that it takes an hour to do so your

hourly risk of dying in a traffic takes the bongo
    flips fistfuls of warped coins, crash while
        driving say that each year you do that two
hundred ways to be like some ice vented my
    street scrounges a face back, some feet,
        teeth made of plastic, arrogant loss of life
expectancy flutters through a head spilled open
    to suggest you cannot, desperate for consummate
    love alone, match that total risk.

SEX CRATER

Lick the gag and lascivious flame fades,
I am shut it goes. Fastened to, snapped
shut by and stuck on her. She makes
up my life pitted for one instinct, see how
does this continuously, rubber shreds
and scandalizes the chewed glass the car
head out through the windscreen.
Her face goes on my leg. Broken
ice scattered in molten chrome glows,
            falsified the compact
            body you bargain
            away chip-eyed and wasted,
            so drunk the
street in an invisible ice-storm and
men and women entranced to a death-fad
go about nothing unheard. Delete the
exit every step of the routine reinscribes,
make a fresh end, link the shadow
vomited from the eye to an erotic highlight
went shut. Moth versus spaghetti: it
says here shut the thing open to greased
suggestions to the same contrary,
            as trusted the light shies,
            waving across
            her face and my single
            is a hit. But forever.

A BREAK FOR TWO

The furtive present debars our collapse; our frangible
atoms quit nothing for which they are too destined;
fabulously gashes in the street gray of ceaseless
yellow from our sun lapse; wow they are again prosperous.
Ethel takes a few Audios, several Creams and mixes
these with numerous Bingos; for Barney several
Creams and then as many O.P.s, they swill each
whirring upon that, can't you sit fucking
still gapes at her, no way she leaps her face off you
try that replies then, neither wishes suddenly to vomit.

Popcorn blinks on Tammuz who wheedles serenely
into the queue for the lobster floss; periodic
universal conflagration, okay and what else also
and why not too, our bleeps ping, each link in the chain
smoking faces unbent flops; Audios Barney make
the air rip you shredless, everything could wow vanish
as boredom can and quiet vanishes, where
you hear squawks, you hear whispers or hear diversible
pledges I hear tyrranic fire raise you, far out
cancelled faces shine, hear rings of destroyed scission.

Barney the Creams and all my tongue is veers,
can't fucking speech alter yours this way never,
gob went ablaze stratopathic, I clean chew
right through the taste of apathy into revolt
should ban disposition, the savour of pensive head flips
dissever equally and bond onto reaction, I excruciate
the zero failing that, see in my teeth wow flings
of Ethel pyro lustre gaze at my creamy lips now
fuck my face away, can my gums sop up magnificently
forever do you think back my tasty descrambled life.

Alongside shopfronts, a changed wow Sisyphus once
for all cavorts and lost his job to robots. Grab
yourself what fulguration maybe, won't make a mess

on the street blended and stricken with dream,
can otherwise the gray amount to you, Tammuz in
turn retorts and winks like a deckchair bolted down. Bristles
all my tongue Barney is now crying
faintly as the Creams flush out blandness, where his
lips drag through a boasted airway scarlet,
soften them Ethel please, make what is hereafter parity.

They spit and boom, they curb wow fragility are
themselves quite the verge; a spontaneous wick burns
fire to a muck beyond travesty; would each
of them say, we participate so in our eyes, that glow
like shitless animals on the moon of Philolaos.
Down the road drizzled apart boys,
girls and their munched fingers and limbs haywire
snack on the bus. Barney you could yet deride
Ethel says the finale of ourselves, you know what
a fucking downside they are, the Bingos are beginning.

Sky wanks the clouds; a placid shower taps on Norwich;
faces slurp mango Hippocrene; every so often, pauses
which Ethel afire castigates and she routs you
whispers the fuzzy air to the fizzy Texan Parole Board,
should love bide among these like a void thought between them,
like also the objective reality of vagueness, Barney
spunks upon Ethel, for her the Bingos fix wow upon facile
air sliced over them, she can know certainty only
because love finishes indecision certainly, now which like
the bent of a comparison ends with her; she puts her face out.

I see it now she says, flaming in her own free sphere
herself languid riot, quickened the nerve that
she amazed feels squirt throughout her optical wow washes
carped life irrefutably; can winds between us
resolve us you and I, can the arc bend, combining you
ought to feel the sky and grayed tarmac,
cringe in sync with Abhassara, ought to chill out with the insects;
throughout this she leapt through the air at him
one rush like an unbreakable promise, her eyes kind;
the insult she says is everywhere revocable, Barney.

What will Zanu-PF do now? What would Olson have done?
The face of things a universal smile, jaw
cramp says Barney you had better have a rest, the O.P.s stretch
him out until 6.14, his cock abuzz with wow tiny Yangtses.
The net crashes. They banquet and carouse and swill,
the table is laid with space for anyone. Perhaps Mugabe would
become whatever we fancy we are. The torch invades my
eye and face is fading, this could be the time to whisper
everything needed and have them die less alterably,
we may never come down, but also may and watch this space decay.

A COUNTDOWN TO REPEAT

Wait. The choice is disbelieved like the palliative
ice glued into my throat and when acid
say gossip confronts them, tearing apart the real divide
incompletely was a stuck on you
are yourself what faces. Wait. I am behind my back,
reshift of crap outward inexact vague, too
sideways to clutch at to recollect when to you
fabulously hate looked made up. Now improbable
light shines, heat itself melts,
in the drafted amnesia do a withstood picnic wait in
fleshy tones and relaxed in time and
        and cold glare blindingly over
        that windscreen flips, distorted
way out like mutual trust. The leaves are all
paranoid, crunchy and when you pick lapses
gone to hate nothing can fix. What among this
strip of things to break draped in my
face is broken at all. Wait. This is a question, can
it be where disconsolate and breaking
faces all are, pitted within the wait thread to finish
you as days can. It was the contract in Bahrain
that Harken won through Bush, who then
admitted its directors to U.S. foreign policy
        meetings of minds
        deranged as an abacus made out
of ice balls and electrical wire, please can
I recover myself hurt whit-boy. The leaves are
rehanged, unconturbated maybe dianoid all
the stars pop. You're so jammy. Wait. There
make that thing. I am extraordinarily
happy alive. I went out and found new people
excited beyond went out, found new
people what they are never that. In the end,
when finally the tangs are slick you
        see finished lights on and
        people you love in a smashed queue.

DO YOU BLOSSOM

As the chosen form of panic car
crash to my rear frozen
out by words too beautiful to spot
are you alone, take off your
chance to wheel through
clouds in unvanishing havoc up
the street in the love
        people too no
        end alone
chancing apart them
and far lived you fetch for
the last time another
night positioned over the lilac
and nothing and bake
you shift out of the wrong window
pellet to a drop end
        life each
        strapping day but
and the ice is gluey so
and the volcano rain is gateaux
far to the way differently
seceded can you taste how
aftertastes vanish outside the rain
in fact chooses to hit rock
bottom on the list of
        uses the break as
        mere toyish
shift to go being on with
and the people to the left
hand side of their own faces bleed
helpfully and ponderous
ash like a whisper steers
immediately the correct heat in you
through no hoop, I love you.

AN ACCIDENTAL ELEGY FOR GATT

Several nights over the apart lounge tags along
caches of foisted dust were people swerving
to each other can you cry still a blank countermand

draped on celery pending are what you cry out
love echoes under the bridge over the motor
way in a straight line foisted to hoax opposites

purple is successes of a melted grate blanker all
new talk of sachets comparable are wetting
and wresting your face you who the dynamic

reply you care for are they and people some
clips of the time off better swerving not ready
made to be tolerable grease and love echoes

into the steadycam nights weeks you break
off never which sachets delete bar overalls
elsewhere new sneaks run off by heart so

what so far non-nondescript hope agitate
pending several can ready you cry up nothing but
in the end makes your hair and teeth drop out.

AMONG THE GOLDEN SHEAVES

In what upreared assent soever
        smothered frozen linnets
trip and chuck, over and out
        the lay they rent out

no the frosty flurry
        of all arch dissuasion I need
not say does not
        echo or often ease

the strain of a little bill
        by all means necessary
not to amble by
        them not a maudlin retort out

choose this for them
        right little discarder
it makes you hang on
        cue an honest terror of happiness.

THEY OFFER YOU SWEETS

Sun sinks off the coast of Portsmouth. Local bus
        schedules collapse. It is okay
dealing a little smack, the petty
        cash echoes through in beaten
up parkways, like your friend calls you
        up, float a while. No person
should beaten and bleeding cry out, leave
        me alone, I am too young,
the light cast on that is impoverished. Smoke
        is a way of life rises
wishy-washy to zeroes overhead, runs out
        from his flat terrified
childishly that fire could shred it and his visible face,
        do not wish to hurt him
alone you drag misery out, instead cut back
        free their rages blind
them to fire always. And so make the shore too incessant,
        no edgy sea, but
alone the slope low shoved pushed down to a dark
        base, insoluble
garnish of dark sand underneath where
        vision must be defunct.
It is the financial cowardice of a democratic government,
        turns them over, fucks them.

INSOMNIA

With a neat smile, hurry
light up and fashion it dire,
        can you believe what I can
you hear of scrub your sea peer
        sunrise, how sewed in that
disgust into resting even cleaned,
        stoned, there is the same add daytime
ripped by wanks and were shreds
        of it daily you were flinging out
is the truculent teeth rip through sugar,
        no wait, in the car stay
stay your hand, be a drag or, paling.

Or two. Together, we
always remember to say love life. To soar
        bird, to skip off flatter in
to clarified air, as you do but competently.
        Rub our eyes, let rip
in perfect time, on the head nail. Stop
        counting the letters drift,
what we see is a day topped up to carry
        gazes away from
day emptily feasible, should slit into my
        slit my wrist and pick out
from in there, filthied a bright disc.

I dreamt that we were standing
side by side by windows.
The light there was a lemon blue,
the stop of your head brushes away shadow.
Drifted poppies on a lawn
you felt for my smile. Now only you could
see, in its reflection a fresher
taint for that window, a neat seeing,
throughout a neat colour of rain we count
off its fall. We two stood there together,
then walked out there, two
feathers as I thought real our first step
by step into no communism.

COLLECT YOURSELF

That at least is something, rubbing your
face in the truncheoned ice
cream less light is corrupted more accept
more alone, what you

say you are echoes out, a moral chin
yours, scripted flesh-out
when the problem was raised they in
tune were unique opposed

fuck off and brigades of whereas
might say dispassion not
a great deal to pick among could
I even when implore

to separate the dots, the gashed
out tepid fire reasoned
face just a faintly and squatless
that is the door, that is the way.

CUT TO LENGTH REQUIRED

Less excluded through that spark
in you could I thrill must
I keeping on breathe ice out in darkened
habit perpetuate the waste of lust
your life shines, also incomparable
drop to
              smashed me in the knees,
pushed you up against
wanted the money to get high on
glue or free, I now for love famished
will breathe even flattery like
the air loved sex confiscates. Do you
can you catch wind of this, in
this are you lived about likewise
stopped, will you make it
up to yourself through squeeze out
me from your life and again trusting
your life
              again lustful, and in
that trust fly from less excess, to a qualified
cock give your tongue gently and in
turn are loved gently undefied
by now the resist switch, the remote
list of what this life is pinned
to the wind broken down and leaking in
to my throat like a stilt. Do you first
craze for detachable. It starts out you
first then Palestine caressed shouts
and gone in the head, then again
Palestine, then the touch of you resulted.

BULLET LUBE

Were shut up and grim celestial
            winds now cracked by
Guatemalan toy-fire, inches ablaze up
            everywhere see to
that darkness got them scavenged out
            yet for your face nearing,
I can break a hatch down too,
            bypass sublimely or
Paki spread your legs I'm blue
            white red and zero
patches my grin up, so what
            next to eat you quiz, e.g.
how did my head get stuck into this
            mock up of transitive
paradise greased to a shadow; from which
            eyes can peck at
anything goes their ad, I want
            three blonde twins with eczema,
immediately, or insteps ratified ergo
            novel fire inflow to drain
magnificently our sky of all darkness.

RHAPSODY FOR THE ENFRANCHISED READER

In the still of adrenaline, the creep of irate
                stars across a clouded tryst
over your head forever, in the farthest
                fetches of intent ambivalence
down upon Idumea, upon pallid Dover,
                where the transcendental synthesis
on standby whirrs on, where additive
                sea butts and sweetly bashes,
a sopping coup for pilchard and sentiment,
                beyond then into the credible heartland
brimstoneless, a rosy haze over
                extinguished pitch heaps, and the streams
thereof in fixed dreams of less
                forgettable amnesia, in the street, here
and / or now, where together we commit this freedom
                a standing order, hereabouts loitering
predicates can shiver, and each looks up like a child,
                and each singly dreams
unagitated, of a job in the Iceland ice-cream sector.

RITALIN DAIQUIRI

I'm as passionate as the next
way I discounted a stab in my forehead
get void of all wiped of all omit
the next way never to break up
and expedite sorrow, then be
alone vague
                    a crisp on
                    ledge by that
do you take the crowd at face
can a fuck glorify and as
tremendous as they are all the related
facts they are blur don't bring
them up one
bring them up one
                    at a time
                    better spent in
you damaged and
rejoins the whole erotic affront
star as yourself in alien bingo
alien washing up little do you
alien alien and later we began all
decreed iron on,
                    heat
                    of you on
me there was a tenderness I
wild to cry for I pick
I did cry broke the body undetachable
was not therefore hateful,
it shone with you keeping my heart
you were keeping my heart
                    you kept
                    warm, there
nowhere the sultry blizzard in
my likes and disowns
spat from you fakes hallucinates spits
from the ground we are can a fuck

waste my time can time waste
my love I ask you everything
                    and this too
              bang

BY PORCHLIGHT

On the street see: further commerce in hatred
of the waning edge, so they slide
over and grip output slides up nobody has
to do what they don't, want to
                        do you make this plain as day,
were that just window wishing. Plain
as nights also scissor, and centrally our bleeps ping
all switch the mute on, edge out
fashioned by zeroes. It's easy as this: get out while
                        you can radishes
in the egg slots, chaos. The edge can
just be obsolete and not waning and why
not. My retro centrepiece. Only a long, hard stare
she said will pop this zip, switch the finical
                        massacre to gray don't
gape you seem retarded. As the news seems
at the edge of my government,
Nigerian pipeline outburst, rain here flushed
slick grimaces away, and every window
                        sill was runny and shines.

SCUNTHORPE MON AMOUR

British Steel today went Dutch my love,
the verbal dead sea won't get me down,
freshly cut the field between trial and
error my whole life can traverse partly,
a small part for most women and men.

The steel of my nerve also is brightly
cashed, stab the mogul. In sullen or
subtle pleasing phrases I show hereby
steely to breaking point, how I outdo them;
trial and error are the climax of this cameo

flesh in the halted turmoil of reasonable
passion for veracity, speeding
despite that halt, in the field as cash.
Suffer a quiet hand to shade your
gaze in its gesture love, for Koninklijke.

DELETES SEX

None too exasperated penis, arise to
the cloud smoked out wire scrubbing device
minced-up fire and lost filed
minutes in dreamt-up oblivion, a throat feeds
this again and again edits wish-lists
                                singular take the very best
                                put first vaseline
don't you tear me like a script. As get drunk,
a way pins and tightens, you that way are
happier caressless shank out, you too bendy
face shoveled on a head. Ironing
bed-sheets, lacquering them as can moonlight,
                                in the way blocked
                                drains keep filthy
rain out and shine alive I press my
teeth through wasted time to your pretty cheek,
caress your ankles and throat, then pull down
steer wheel miss out on collision,
a small melodrama of tarmac and now punctuated
                                face ripped off
                                the cuff you recommend
peace, dialogue, a new end to shot-off mouths
tongue cut by bite-size, too freed
speech slurred out clipped out, our sticker from all
glad use freed, and again the complaint is inevitable and
parallel to the news each propped on the table
                                switch ffwd. anus
                                to heart come in
did erupt like change fails. To happen
at all so the script. A young boy shot in the face by
what right screams. Come on shit-face off
your mind on snorted vanish rattle your
head the biscuit-tin, snap out your throat
                                this more do often
                                would like to see you again
eyes sliced into shelves put then eyes on
these shelves whisk and paste them look at this

proposal to cut tax. It does what it says on
the burnt-out arab lips read out on
the dinnertime news like a joke slurred,
                        in kissing you perfectly,
                        wanting you
to love my face. Sit on like a buckling fence
which won't crack up you crack up
you brush your teeth off you switch off.
I'm not the person I never used to be. Such that
outside, the disillusioned bank sprays cash on
                        so creamy
                        accepted wind licks off
tanker windscreens which all squirm twist orgasm
and yet, are bland. The secret is to delay for
as long as you are. To negotiate a dismay flap,
and the pressed stoical and oh get up cancelled in
to the trash-compactor shouts a debate
                        runs through the grotesque
                        chisel list cut
in toothpaste with a Mars bar. But, we can
make love. And, we make love. For a buck we can make it
leap through a hoop. I from the script hurry to edit out
your breast, feet-paint, beautiful hair-cover,
lust after justice for lips-gear scalpel batter
                        me rip me stop
                        altogether U.S. beating
blood out like your smoky heart. And then she turned,
enunciating: "The procedures of the laboratory
tests render the concealed infection visible
and meaningful to the scopic technologies
of epidemiology and some other bureaucratic
                        surveillance practices.
                        I am not mysterious."

THURSDAY AND FOREVER

The street rate more feasible is cylindric,
continuously the visible subjection fails
to disappear of ourselves to estranged,
mutilated sincerity, as however the backdrop
rises to clinch you hopes thrash about,
I cannot begin to disclaim how most idiotic
wishes I have thin, they screw up like
crepe and easily burn. As faraway I wish
parades through my eye disheartened,
at the petrol stop, that the agreed tremendous
corrugated flight into Parliament should
eradicate you fool, every branch of indirect havoc
gouge out fitting room for the medicated
solid infection you are if too late
discuss that combined anyhow, I see basil
in the windowbox lilts. The storm they
are created passion, people each ran into what
had faced conjecture off and burned this,
twitches, takes back her hand. Could we now
each sees myself descried as always inside
flamboyant neutral bodybag of air and rain,
teeth habitual so face of you, so alert fixate,
so they said the power cut. I cannot believe
that the U.S.A. hadn't provided for this,
sneers at the bang away outside and falls
down time destroyed, where became of
my perfectible love for you, you my
intensity has serenaded that fades, in a corridor
way broken remarks distribute everything,
each cassette of sleep is live, the forensic
regiment of dreadful love and copy
will you base Belgrade on the whole thing
this evening. Wishes flock to across
possibility in a flash of quiet they take
viciously into your buying power and die,
six cloudy feet to the back rubbish.

Pace yourself to the dead centre of that riot,
I reflect on the street edge. And of embraces
such as these now querulous ask nothing.

As life were or were not

     put by distemper inter

mixed beyond claim or

     my correct order, move to

remantle gently; be where

     always and the turn from

always lately gives in

     tact benefit. Still be

lied by life the slight

     purview beside

you says you

     fit throughout, where

finally who knows, is us loved

MINCEMEAT SEESAW
Fit A

To evade cinereous ice which cut
              back repro were they set
up for retraversing as
              if incomparably or mute her
skips a beat, recall it were the attached
              remit-plaudition to faded
trust to appear refreshed, her for
              skips back put allayed in
stantial, should there ever be
              come back as a choice, now I adore
her will not be remote fast to
              hide which cut
remark that, age of my stray through honey
              suckle and flaring
rayon to put undercut said probate retrans
              mission to sink
a fortune, angelic edicts scattered and bent
              on a rise in fine
mind and clemency set up put tract
              able to sigh scoured fire, wink
out at her, grazing
              her wrists, on ice:

slowly the park is colourless
        it should become that
re-entered way, not and of to begin
        with more to begin with you
should hear say a bent put by, no way were that what just
        inside its own stayed
flare you'll ask to freeze, high vacuum
        conditioning to a crass jot all in
rate-saccharine stop how stop how put
        by does her
the park is flashing does
        her
terror die on in shoved hypo pigeon self-help self left that die
        in vs cash out ab-hypo
respite they should all be alert
        I can see the sea-waves converting
I am torn by a contentless anxiety
        pink and yellow, top end
rasp caving in stop or put by gristle reflac my heart's on
        fire and ice redound
if you may now to her to her now do not stop
        we were pleased with the news

stayed in a received zephyr, fair
zephyr I shall trust shall iron and irresolute
                now flickering,
pegged in trust sit to reset no hear out is an honest gale
                is screeched famine is too
scorched cuts too pay up too fast
                to deny for her
it does all this we see clearly to concur we see pay how
                put by, received heed-stack
one to two the rift there thank you within which
                fair zephyr, newest rated
zephyr elides with pain, again say and proving anew pay where
                a blustering, real famine it is
trust in trust in a rift real rift fair
                minded legal fact-attaching here
goes she shall see her terror at her
                feet now glazeless daylight floods the sky
I am in love and apprehend the earth do not gain subtlety
                you, fair zephire
to zero repay here goes put a wisp of hay register yet another
                dying bootless nigger

started to rain then must get obliged to go
            on to the go on route sallying
rooks at bay they do notice are as contrite too late they notice
            love under the drill, so sunk
base beneath their clatter arrested break off gaze
            up at a rising
sky, levelling
            whisper; to gasp
proof that I am
            to lie is
another lie flan debit mash liability obliged to prevent cabbage stuffed up
            high as the swindled stars can be
are now with just repressive ease, twinkling
            by me as, I ask
break were there storm outside would then say on be proof
            were light on at her heel, advancing
calmly at access recession on in via stay which contrived
            need for a lowest care
could slide and blur down rate super-astro I love you

circa moderate L.E.D. tocsin
utter darkness, all together we had approached in
saying which I
all together we were stop my mouth
is full can't were hopeful we
had hoped to approach, to a fanfare
from a blaze just skipped out had the right turn
over and trust still full over had
we done this
she asks, I frown at the fireside pane and smoke
idles out of her
budget alarm break on put wasp-incut by as little
to do through the playground, the intercepted letter
of the Abbé Guyot on our minds we
were approaching had
more time did
choking in enraged
hope stay with us for for
ever step up money down step
down pay up stop flat:
I am content with a contentless anxiety,
cobalt and indigo, see the sea-rudders

I, Keston Sutherland, am from the royal dale
                from here within which we may watch
out at the sleep and dew blitzed
                weeks one two watch sit as a united put
down to put up with
                held her to sit at we did it all go on to crouch
at to infer a watch set, no relief
                for those for whom the taxes are fated
sweat spurting from down in those people
                do say barbaric seely
lilt of the crossbreeze just where
                it is in between what you find just
ice and crimes of toy fire convert to a deft plain
                hope and what time
was it I
                had better be on
my part
                I am twice loyal

not cattle at fear deposit here too tautened grades of bright
           pollen see disaffected swaying
out of hand shot pollen see
           not pollen please trust
me too I'm scared
           there is an opening in prick garnish
she is a part of this
           storm put out snapping in
place I was buying cocaine it
           from a friend I
too part of the destiny
           of fen drainage circa 1641 here
too, here, as I am, not
           cattle not see not put cracked in
pollen-sea gay wave upon
           she is alert now
she has been alert the whole time, please sit
           down and still, now, and hear
what she should like to say: ait
           enim iram esse cupidi-
tatem doloris reponendi
           splash out on your cunt-chaw and fuck off

here upon peace data to rely
          let your grip drift, down
stream and there to the side not
          idle contrary perfusive there
will be less
          to break
you do you
          hear listen, lapping
there will be less
          we put this
to the executive stayed by a new iron
          reflex and can shift
much as like but
          rust in no peril
I am relying
          just elsewhere on despotic brutism,
as are you,
          ink pig

                    waved her fingers as he left
through to same pattern wanted too
                    much be casual she
whispered goodbye put
                    aside for an ambition
there was appeal a precept a by credit-transfer it did
                    not fail
her life which
                    day speeds by most
gradually would you say by waved her emptied
                    fingers, for the level
evening, it had run
                    as glue in acid his
shadow speeds by and by
                    grades dissembles she
stands alone, and in her door
                    way is placated, waving
bloke shut up nothing is not shattered
                    less than less
life down flat at hold fast as a spare rung
                    set her
eyes run over, as he sped by
                    waving back and sighing

smear my eyes with oil then waft
lid up down crack cover my
face it matters
flea-head there's nothing she likes more than not than a
rent my throat out
side there's gnat fission to other people teeth waft
up down rot out that is
her favourite nothing more people you
say yes other
lip snaps up is glossed it matters, too little
to lay about better
moving nothing better she is my favourite
lease my tongue she
is really my pill divides up they are
all starving it's
raining out it what it other you say yes your
right in display, sunk
other flea-head
several scraps of drift-food
head for rent she
has a favourite, I shall waft
it matters my lid up
down it's me

with global badger-tetanus and high full with wild
            roses hangs the
earth in the wind high
            loves its wonder
collation shut up put out swipe put up temper reset
            I know what's going on I know what's
going on I know what
            scrap no excuse, where
are you
            fusing your snitch stayed what
are your eyes to your repeat hands
            swiping today sir goat-dissent
I am in love for the world is a mild shadow, inside
            which is the way
from itself battery
            prawn farms on the coast of India
repeat rape
            rape rape rape
rape rape nothing
            much to do
with you
            boy this or that wednesday

closed in to what all you liked scant not often,
        came upon a pale face to sync beaten,
all about that tender place no vile thing
        too soon in soon perishing;
valued in part at large the dream for this,
        tender still may distort at pit-pat ease those images,
night of my say and say to rest
        that so it may I trust;
the pale face is to wear out love me further,
        notice of my dream by a place one way tender
or the other and still in for retort competent,
        regard the police are weeping away

Fit B

Sun's up and we're what's breaking out in warmth what's
                what easily said so
what I heard this sexy Russian free
                fall batters world market, breezily played
and pliant in the obsolete prolixity
                of shade and ashen
visages squint it up pack zero dilate do you
                need more time flash
back with your eye-glint set alert your pegs in
                to the earth of this premier bio wait I
I see a numb love, at
                rest at
plodding
                down
I see a
                shutting my eyes, I
at war
                do not disturb
that rag in the ditch which smothered in Tesco
                own slash-price lo
ving sunray
                62.7 drop
5,399.5
                shop til you learn
to stop
                bogey-boy here from say wank cut cut cut

was a peachy rise in the mock
up net addition to productive
                capacity we swam through the air
all night, fixed as a groat
                and pelted with kisses to a ploy supple
so far no but hacked out distract renew you
                know death is nothing
but a trump splinter of aggregate supply we
                streaked throughout the night
straight up put pelted with
                all through
the night repeat check pin not
                too fast too what no I too
little to make iterative, all through the night
                a blessing I am to my own,
only semi IRA,
                semi tinned mackerel

On a Jut at the Cape of Good Hope
            cannot yet despise with a baleful
eye too slimfit
            each unresanctioned
shifted inch of to placid
            minds a breathless empire under these waves
each twitch of straw get
            out in time each caw and trill-less
this veto what can
            call it you should prejudice
I cannot yet disburse at a feckless cut
            back repro rate rate what rate rip
grin into place disburse it softens
            there on the incline, inset, in
good time bossing and sobbing can
            not disburse or despise well
what did
            you expect put spun and saw geen
uitgang rook
            verbode put out
I cannot trust I am young I hey plug in connect gust
            to game for a change
of heart at a choice
            of planet slimfit opt-bin
were surveying the daze of drought at the tip of these waves
            which clash and bellow, a rota
dismissed re: circumspect contrition bash up, few scattered
            kids and their life hop
by and berate as
            you may you may
buy your love for them bulk,
            cosmo inverse rehab
say it could be for the choice of nothing new

little pennons on their heads which rotate as they trot
                Lesotho Lesotho
permanent vacancies positions
                vacant hinweggegangen I'm
I say I'm I am
                not to desert put
where mouth is your
                each component undulation set in
no fever reset scam to perduce I see
                the sea in ah waves the birds
in sky ah just
                one second you these
people where stop their bonus stripped
                softly from her ever restless
positions vacant no
                rustle no option not
to buy for the ear buy
                what did I say that's
right,
                rotate

                    I wanted to capture the whole world,
to be what will coerce
                    and had I failed, had I to want
a drowsy nettle idles wholly
                    ought be more calm were
swimming
                    we free at heart
a day pings out
                    quick burn intermodal connive get
nowhere must
                    stop must I hurt get
set make the whole
                    world captive with your option
but have not turned
                    in time,
did not pick trust did
                    lulling the scraps of attempted patio, we all
wiped out better you
                    said it and say on the nail you fix on
I would like to join in
                    wanted to fail forever

                    so far round and round about
my love to spare and not lick out,
                    about assignated and can break
free or bend free once
                    pauseless, always
then tattery,
                    uh-huh but
to yet conflagrate in advance pearl-eyed,
                    retort tiny slit exceed,
and so the swap and sway of flame
                    for flame headed put do sit up
at denting ice
                    still, if you break you pay,
still, I'm rubber for fifty points
                    and you get two

a sigh of snow falls in
differently upon my patience I am at
rest it's
low in the sky and for this legitimate, frozen in
safety from panic
and upon
forgetting this I
too a feat of treason
new friends London Paris New York
call out to your friends
new names go by
so, a sigh of snow falls
say a sigh
and all the rebate forecasts are trapped / battered in
tonic sobriety taken for
a fat lot of
what
it's never not and nor
is much else choose this
tip-top rape-jingle

a secular upward trend in vapid glee
           as flowers their idle sweets exhale, relays
love to the fathomed packhorse so-and-so,
           the bees drowse out, investment peaks and suds
of gayer prattle pong from washed-out mouths,
           the grace of trended variables to be borne
not of yourselves, nor yet to tease awry
           the flat-out frown and all it militates
in favour of as wrapped in plastic rags
           an Afric baby slender as an elf
sidles in picturesque sedition, in
           time to the beat of the fist in your heart which sprung
open reveals the grip you achieve on love,
           as you see fit to lunge at it, timing a gag in the dark

saw the candour dwindle, softly
           whispering upon a flame
wherein of these neither
           abates though both weigh
one gnat and career
           as it may see
it flutter, swaying
           for instance I can see
to it to see saw fear, desire
           ramify pelted upon approach fled out bickering
one put candour one put can shut
           up to a peak of say, candour
sucked and blent in a bin full of wasps
           into summer, and at our liberty
purveyed saw the rapid
           start here
nothing before it's neither
           a lie to abate nor cut
out, what you can
           trembling gently upon candour
must then be beneath you

took the floor shrieked in reply to expunge trust
                    three or
four daubs less
                    horror may
you'll agree be fit
                    idiocy to this end quit
as only you may daily
                    and from one real
moment to the next
                    recant decoy quit / found
herself to be sniffing
                    out my heart one
notch to the next and no trust
                    leaked, put I swear
tonic in soft out
                    or burn up to the twinkling sky part
inert and police by-product
                    to soar there vacant
but would I lie
                    down to this end fit in panic out flapping
rebel tongue in chirpy
                    despair through a pint of TFP, moonlight
sloping against the out
                    cast issue of hope
errands as I trust
                    you too shall ape of the total spin

           alert in a song view to scattered
confetti to seem remote trot way past
                worry no
loss of insight out of sight so seem remote or out see proven
                distance flocking in, to forfeit
first lapse in noble annoy too brief
                you wail, and let you fall
to stacking the inches
                dreadful calamity
wedded to a vow in blue fire, go on put
                me out, my love can I ache to
there may not be a revenue
                in this alert, busted and tottering
by and down the bend
                of a naked street, for a clad proof
taken by
                Taiwan by numbers
sing this vow
                what can this song vow be

placid gape a friend and sure
              fire gain in
real love,
              trundling
up to a high view
              reject mezzanine (A) to pang out get
together you
              may
just these seconds
              or so ago (B) have
leapt to note just
              this, take a break
Bukharin there is a minibar in my brain
              and I will elect
you by me all
              brothers to
sisters and back again,
              otiose rebate faucet
gripping out
              of the placid ailing question,
weeping (C), hinder this forfeit should you
              may be happy in
your turn and still
              the leisure you regret,
outsourced, easy as that

Fit C

That day the rays through cloud racks broke
                in and in time their careless proof
all placed about
                me startled, candid
soft regret even tires to erase this, plain when I ran
                alarmed in a rattle of faded
shade and repression, from a woman,
                stop
I have it both ways
                can she deride this perfectly,
batting lashes coerced crime descriptor
                I will make it all fit
when I ran
                out able and alarmed, battered
out the downward redress autarch static
                fist in the sunlight, both ways
clipped apart and ruses
                spilled at a gutter end,
that day
                and day to day
and daylight
                some day they are permitted

on the face of the season on my way here
         you may compare them
the face of everything
         the hazel and white-thorn
sycamore, lime and ash
         at York, ripe walnuts
bricks
         percussive softness, within
a mile and broke into fine hills and shadow
         today it is in the north
clear sunshine but cold
         but made fresh shoots
and shall continue the best ever
         their person had not betrayed them
betrayal is far greener
         with such a year,
and your care is odious,
         vile, though not betrayed

few arid between rain slits open
            called a blank, thereon
set her foot
            Paris was usual so between hot rain by wind
carrier and a dozen
            hostages fried wherever
there was fierce debate, wailing
            back she tore in
half a mind at
            me where
wind quits this quits, later we set back
            to love and I drew
it with us, over
            a bridge and flew past the lobby to
bed and rode me, softly
            as I would your willing ear
might crave a new world static,
            new breakdown,
newer blackout

were indeed it to be, that free
of my idle dark regress, a shimmering
            fall in my power
to stop as
            I alone might left
me hurt where every
            hurt and every repetition, stung
quick and still
            yet here,
and yet brightened, and O were a frail
            deceit alone
to bait these, hurt
            and repetition which only
fail as a joyous cry
            to what was life may disowned in a new
wind raced down through
            over flattened tar broke
and happy to the coastline,
            where before returning,
and I could hardly
            breathe at
point you made
            me amazed
and joy so
            alone you sent this query, love

sag along the Milthrop turnpike four
miles straight down
the lane to left calmness
brightness calmness
roar of the waters, five miles
saw the forge the Dæmons at work
by the light of their own true
fire trailed by
beat into bars and plates
and brightness, calmness
Burton to Lancaster
news o'erhung
I even slept to
night in peace despised assuaging
panic in azure blowtorch wafts put
scattering pallid glisters,
novel shadows about the wharf-side
but you a little disorder
in their position
you ad libitum like
Khayelitsha come no fixed
hysterical
contrition six
miles five miles up a warm
and finely dappled
airspace
analyst warmth / dapple forecast from which
metal may rain out numbered
as your days yet over
look your hours evade this

as we cannot build to raise are stricken in
                breath to a novel fire
sound, from trust at my heart
                it raised, so put can I too cap
my fire with miserable dust
                as only thus I may calm
now and
                plainly alive
faggot
                juice of the pandemic ultra
my little island here
                Ascot bleeding gums
wait for it to crash in
                and bellow sic recall from
trust bellow said at my
                heart gag at as
we cannot thus I and cower at sagging slit of dawn
                rip requited to all acid novel
bland and slender
                courage to turn in time, all
flash in all always and forever plainly
                pathetic to fail exhort you

                    slander fares in a lay
as her wrist in strip
                    of lint for the clear and easy shadow
does not fail,
                    and a break of day from
day so brittle is easy and clear
                    sleet pale in the vanished driftway
settled and then into a brightened hour
                    for what good manner of disbelief
quick retraction era or a winter
                    to sanction for what sudden prick
of guile and scarce flair,
                    sea-wave, song-blue, sea-change
I sit smoking emptily
                    I am in love
and love is a militant acceptance,
                    the lambent slander of a shadow

                    for and against celerity
inflow of the magic forest
                    don't titter but slap up a list
crossed swiftly what to bounce
                    what matter or slip out cast
down or unable to snivel before I fly
                    the desire a thrush I
am and need
                    a cigarette Congo uranium celery
a wavering chisel a life
                    line on line and avidly
sketching a blank should cut
                    this out now
and then get proud and aggrieved, to whisper
                    to whisper the free
cure of infracted loyalty
                    is dearer, or dearer for me
than the self
                    catholicon of its obverse velleity   .

another light show and Israeli avocado
                in the morning my life
is a cunt how are you
                go Chirac go
off the boil as I do
                break my head in out in in sad
soft self deposal for
                what fix of entrained alarms
our heavy our cruise our barrage
                milk it have
a go pinch a line
                their silver coats reflect
the dazzling beams (GAY), the harvest
                scrolls to a blazon icy to
mind as a wood-faced tin
                pot plastic iron willed retort,
from a rubber demon, he only who can say
                fire
ping
                pop
pow
                we must destroy this monopoly, now

this blunt line is a resource sleeted under
                    say did you spend your pastime
nose to the wild flower, to wind
                    up with what left
over in damaged and tossed about by
                    nothing to prate for a bind
gulled to purple year, to yearn
                    up the scavenged
banter accounted for sullen or put by
                    carefully this to remind
broken the pretty ear, not
                    dread too much a real chance out set out
perfectly, I could her
                    hair or what
rusted spade too
                    gannet I could be
trustful now, were florid
                    wild to rise
up to greet for
                    all my very spare indifference not too out
of mind tipped but apart
                    so sorry, for what my chance
had settled as, can I be sleeted under,
                    still this is the near blunt cover upon that
and yet run idly I exhort the sea-covert

it is a robust world, and such
a robust earth and not afire, pivoted
                nowhere to stare
out magnificently, and with a roaring glaze
                at daylight which robustly
inward cannot fall, nor ever shall my heart,
                it is too robust were a face
off either to trap in to pincer by, yet my own great
                dread should not ever fail, I have far
too nerve for this, it is yet ever rancid default
                intransigence and to floods out
far to cheapen real death even laced
                in brain with piss coke-mash not a word breaks
near to even against this I ever will
                pivot to stare and collide
with nothing afire, we must never triumph,
                you must never either

                    put to the floor, which sunk
out and stuttered may so uplifting
                seem and be that truly too, aware
awaits the term to deny this, it's
                you or me and the sun
sets up in a ponderous flash wait for
                ever so quickly and on
what, for what to be finished,
                yet what's more
to come is always fair, hear flutter
                a secret receipt at the grate
no rash jot too late scratched-out I'm bar
                barren fire zero wait do
you see that, and everything must
                go and everything
stays to
                fro or sweetly
swaying between, and yet to stay
                is never either, cannot be put a sea-cut
such piteous jokes and faces passed
                up and away and ahead, to stay
is a rising fall from the dead.

**Poems collected as
[Bar Zero]**

A LETTER TO BRITISH AEROSPACE

You were the grand directio more
than a scuffle would surely grasp this,
throughout see the weeklight
come to zero raise your hand now
            and then even, and not how
grasped but how ungrasped it may
itself seem is the startup delusion.
Even-handed I see this,
the screw-up pallor off which snap trashy
            no-hope codes you
snap up at the first commission to sigh,
hope too can be excellent. Though the earth
may on the daily skids tilt
as usual at nothing nothing wraps up
            peace with a grosser
ribbon of pangs than this, that
the question should so slightly run
so coarse an errand, only between hope-codes and no-hope,
itself smoothed and made you will it
            run out or, not and

well who cares. When in New York I ran
inside, when unbusy I aspirin
too much and just run out the coked-up garment
district wow myself blaze-boy
            could chewed up lights
spat stars out. To my heart streets to nowhere
together saw that slid in
and the sky was thin and everywhere magnificent,
thin faces acheless I went blurry,
            you are the bar-zero you eat
everything and later it's dark. As if it
were dark, how could it ever be so, a light
lunch and the grin slots back. We ping.
They're not all like this,
            I alone was the one so tremendous.
Elsewhere hope runs what a quiet

person may call its quiet course;
tottering round their igloo, now tending
the rise of an adequate fire things
          we used to call esquimaux whistle.

I love you, this is a voice from zero-bar.
The codes bright, various you may run among,
this includes the fabulous sky over
and the sky made by metal rains
          a running outtake, and her bright yellow
sun and cerulean stuffed with crab
apples and birdsong served up as dessert.
Were justice a code also. And whatever night
may mean, for sure it
          can't be the sole other menu item.
I wish you could sleep by my side,
literally all of you. Then we might
wake up at the same time, we bold and each leaping
out from a doze degraded now
          to habit, with fistfuls of rubber laurel.
Shrimp run through the Pacific. What is
the time now hope-rated, could run off a sparky
derision true and fireless everywhere
washes the sky back to us, the sky you hope on
          which to put your foot down.

REMARK TO THE WEST WIND

Ring the changes, ring them up,
as the wind in verdict, out from
the sun departed, here throughout
the city runs on faces and windows.

Wind primordial, disordered
asyndeton blowing over
windows and faces, whisper, is this
here remark yet the camp

concentration touching your
invisible acumen? Outringing
in my ears, the serene
brake-screech you might imitate.

LATCHES

You shall be tendering your resignation, pat the debased
        sky at my heels zeroes in,
in a mood-swing on icon of nothing broken;
        birds track throughout it.

They are the fate-codes irate grey and self-denouncing,
        to rubbish as dewy sparkles
underfoot tracks bent and re-bent and go back to themselves,
        and going back with them

you, yesterday my face-coo today all floods and malaria,
        soft taco wednesdays, accepted
words shoved anywhere you. I can say that endless
        regret is that toyish: death etc.

TO THE LAST ANSAPHONE

Beneficent, whose will so slight and even
      yet shiftless by meriting zero must eradicate
          zero and panic would never except
for stunned in the barest gazes clinch on everything,
      this bashed-in is the face I
          too gaze from or at anodyne-face,
and yet zero, yet found by the sleek touch of her
      neck still to be fastened on
          to gro-late auto-craver-me as up top fiery,
repeated, untraffickable outburst goes on razes
      traffic in fire and restates the celestial
          counterpart in a blink and mere daylight.

Beneficent since anything like that
      rhythm of trust or even bashed-in
          greyed preemptive echoes of this turns
no cash midflight, is the 57 channel zero-echo and head on
      any fire to get happiness once somehow
          kissed and my face changed
nothing you see yet wow, what stop brusque
      insta-stop love got stuck
          on my head and lingo got all done-up,
so that a credited passion through I
      think these deadened livid days, seeming
          so wished out may like a soft face brighten.

Lust now merely for what, such as that
      no-one contrives a dead-end and just names
          this the midsequence you skip over
into the sunrise as who did who blinded whom cowboy, by what
      news of more stricken I wince I
          cry me vacantly, fill me in whatever did
zero do to deserve this, so to be held up
      over the sedate riot of yes and no are you

exactly where you are, now,
yes or no, or do in a civil screech we run out pass
by slip from and feign over
all the beneficent life unstopping.

A POW ODE

For a second leave it out purposeless
have I a new run verging heart
pounding the floor flat take
me with you cry out a hit current starry
                    fiery burst out, of
mind completely where you step up,
these are my hopes swapping, pan
fixed to nowhere and out: be mine my
be mine worry studded or she star my
                    be fiery as grey burnished
mine this steel to fling over them cut
on by cut she was the driver brown
fields tore by window saw birds up
trance of me pressed on she drivers
                    take me where I lead for
all my life the passion I screen in, how
do we go, on alive crate by
screen in what purposeless they to
be heard storming craze among us
                    one may stand or wait: trust,
what news is called this: what of
it is you proud, you not sorrowing,
claw of sodden tree part the air to drain
free away, over the wild choked
                    sands the wind you suffer
fall little blinks upon you, "dazzling"
"intense" "dynamite" "hilarious" view
birds wheeling upon the stair cloud by
rote bet you don't get all scruffed up turn
                    out the lights kiss
                    serrated she drove me outside
flutter the green, all turning
connive at been prior of all my life I
was a plain follow what you are taken forever,
can that just have been my
                    track forward be mine, would
                    have it so quit

face breaking red blue mirror grey be love
me too much to nip craved blazing done
for spread right over slit on cheer on
were this my error on, and no mirror finds there
                    passion to show and brighten,
                    all of them do naturally,
look at the person you lean: dark
easy noiseless empty bright noisy
easy covered namibian dazzling make a change
made up change that, intense "fabulous"
                    "suspenseful" "steamy"
                    "intelligent" view
settling your queer apart steady see for
fed nothing can ruin me up, tree
hanging over a mile and broke turning
can ruin what of it is you smiling:
                    burn my face off,
                    scratch out her bland clitoris
swung round you were faintly saying
can be true, whatever all said they do pinching
carried mine off plain away fed
running in of clear doubt ruined driven
                    fields of brown
                    and high lines of clouded
life we stopped and chew breakfast shook
dust from our skins, going by
now forever maybe but hinder
not her but an entire people wasting way
                    later I take
                    my time you can have it
"unmissable" "slick" "fast" "parry"
pity comes at last sews a grasp
on you ferrying in
quickly to or treenight skin or hair driver
                    on time and over
                    all sight, yet nowhere.

Gobsmacked less and less rail in put
out flagrant shining by what you spat
to a token planet and dye

evenly runs upon your teeth upon yesterday
                                upon the streetlife yesterday
young in my scrape, fire in
my way fir under snow and nip out
somewhere above me a hidden trail
to the side blazed, makes run softer lights rubbishy
                                split nail I flung
down on the waving grass in spring,
breeze surmounted, every
thing cops a cut in the price set on
top of the sticker transience has on,
                                so would you make that swayed
for a dash of bronze to pick at: fade
through weeks to fade through, you in
turn they wild are your own
endless Semenovsky Guard of the heart keep
                                on trucking "spectacular"
"epic" "sizzling" "quite" view
I saw her spread a damage so knotted
ends split out to reward in
calm words to strip her off of all that
                                racking my own inelastic
                                give and take your pick:
sun setting mellow crimson, orange
and bright glances rounding
up what shadow fallen
upon yellow grasses they may wane to
                                tonight you are all my own,
                                take from me if I hear
you correctly yelp on, fire: brink
to brink and day, today I see so plainly too
stop turning insight out, what world
may over that clay paste its spell
                                far and writ wild,
                                strip me of my passion up closest,
who can snap contrary yet brink
stutter away who's a happy clay then on
on crab paste sit retching
put on quick the passion in you screen
                                february "human"

                "blinding" "magical"
"trot" view lately the glamour you were
sprung from caramel tint
to memory has it go fun often you
want to put that back in and go away,
                but you never will,
                I'd say if I were you happy
happy as nettles cluttered under pylons,
can my shrug dick out fat change me
the place we would be happy in
is a place in happy hands: view it,
                first with your branded eye,
                coming up next, Xena the gay bat.

Sighing, having, breaching, rank coded
glimpses eyeing the world up, one
can be on top of another
another day flipped to which peep lurching
                did you see I
                cried we all must change,
we must be changed short
breaths catch on spirited
why over persistent maniac dream fire
grate out sorbet to drooled
                to be given freely
                spin or head needed: flag
curving prettily, fluttering by bellowed
verb strings pranking
it to shreds it falls to blankly whomever
blankly you put it on loves you too
                far away where the sun is rising
                light to gather my
profit to see in talented "moving"
"generous" "classic" "dark" view by zero
hazel and currant whack anti and to die
for and sit and blow your top
                rap on her grille
                reach for the star in
livid night detained slid rose and scraped off
hit in the gut's eye by every

subtle season famishing the scum far
tacky but boy did we gaze sing and are wild
                    what can I do,
                    who am I to say quietly,
do I whisper for all of us, the land
sparing my life and fading
heart, will scrawl another jissom
on the desert sand in gore you
                    should be prouder, have a go art
                    curry to fart by
fuck off get your own ideas anyhow
as we were driving right, in nowhere
shone as it could my fashion
of crying out for brightness we both see it,
                    over and done
                    with your permission
cowered and paled where am suddenly
I where do we scoot paled
see you later must be off your mind
flung far again pricks another blink up
                    sun catches the screen fiercely,
                    I will not sway or dream
that you pull over, tree to claw
into shadow a trap we sleep and wake up
in the world clawing
back from garbage hyperion do sever us
                    go for the car
                    or open your trap "non-stop"
"radical" "honest" "Burma" view
cut: the word here is pow,
experience flashes out with it from us,
half the time I leaning to chuck it out
                    is intimate as the echo of too briny,
                    too far wasted, too plain as day side,
trying to hold that the tightened
crate you wholly are vividly to fire
a shadow craving shadows to blend by,
                    fire makes your stand flattened shadow.

SHADES OF GRAY FIRE

Where are the crazes, where the mass out
running of needlessness,
who disobeys the order break free
always and wows you thin

lifed as you are then less then
turned to fizzy syrup breakthrough, there you
go over the same delays have
that extinct panic, stay straight-faced,

for summer clothes that pack like a dream,
for a new approach to nowhere else,
with soft seditious rains and the idle
urge to give a shit or two or else

and the order is barked melopop
oil fails somewhat, is beyond
the rainbow these flagrant shades of gray
were damages faces,

then should I lonely watch them out,
but the damages are craze
control run by remote fact-pushers on you
me and the speech we

breathe deeply alive, stop you don't
slip out we can always lift those
shades and a finger each at the sky orgasming,
gray ablaze, our faces fumes and echoes.

THE CODE FOR ICE

The patch sewn so well anywhere,
due to the relaxed power of insight out washes
and about news to me turbid drip, I was just
saying due to relax echo, inside
                flip and going sour, get in,
get in me sour, how we can ask credit
our mutter banging out, from the earth back
to front to have flat-out earth on autofire,
fuck you once more drearily scanned
                gazing, side to
side long vanished I scatter, get the
hell out I once, more say, say what
ever you feel can, loud and clean
daylight is a blindfold
                RE: further
democratic reforms and political
stability in entrants; improve burden
sharing; increase weapon sales;
dearest light of day you ever
                burn the powered grays
of night to bright crap, here summer is
here again run away me
throw pass up the canderel serrated, better
off than malawi you were kind
                of tired everyone hurts sometimes,
don't they RE: cost savings from scale
economies in weapons production;
foster collective defense capabilities;
adapt to post-Cold War environment;
                croon of her traits and winning eye
lash and of my fire to scrawl set out
breath on alert 2. trap a clarified
angle on time see doubt for the shattered
choir it were, unharmed
                threw the blind down, 3. you
see ice incompletely scolded won't run

through the proper surges
you bash in that glaze in havoc or absolutely
not you at all don't bash, fetching
                coy the deleted sparks
they shone and are precisely due, everything
must go yet you stick
around, for just one night the perimeter
frozen and pale, is of
                yourself too sure as day's
plain and can, forget it
RE: interoperability, can this one hour
flow within our fists spread can
fire be pretty shut, can we see
                the flinch of our ice wrung.

The code does not treat of elements,
my lips are sleetless, torn
cornetto wrappers stick around idly,
daylight bends up on raspberry creosote,
                see just how far
mind that you do, time pops
a clatter of canaries arcs off on mute strap
in love, strap in the light of day pat
the puppy sucks the twix
                freedom is beautiful
twilight ferrying stars to Iraqi
skies in metal descant,
fresh from booth, box and tick
pick a prayer they have
                the flurry of verbs set free
I carried out openly re. parties will develop
separately and jointly their
ability to resist armed attacks; parties
will promote well-being by
                encouraging economic collaboration;
on the bruise, an ice-pack; parties
can request that members consult to review
traits check eye check
told me a tale went something like,
                pleasure to pleasure passes

and the night in grays, new
colours banishing, washes the sight
free, and parity shadowed you
once more can require love
                    yet, free is itself a code
dirt-suffering, you eat the beyond,
outbreak of inner trembling
scruffy face, reek of freedom outcodes
basic ice and click up a Jap
                    schoolgirl branded hot.

Wasps sting a baby and money weeps
O ode of mine you're a diamond,
the cheeks pinching, rubbish
scarlet, try to remain completely visible
                    do I want pee
go-go Honduras in PVC racked
racket of intro, swarms to the beyond
sudden alight, piece by
pieces all the news and I singing
                    into my heart take
I am alone scrap, to worms a pander
flesh careering or
stand tight and sew the patch
of outrage to a hole above
                    my chin dreams are coming true
freedom is not the code; love
free of ice is
of ice, belonging passionately,
you can say free this free that of
                    ice, so what
you say can and will be used
up burned like patent styro cutback
flaring to zero, natter
swung a balloon at sheet eggshell
                    sex on the beach
and love on the blink, things are hotting
up like the fuse in a fridge plug;
the heart gripped like spam by batter;
likeness was a trick we clapped for

                         eye snare, spoon
fed freestyle, to do as we pleasant
shifts in the theatric log may,
but my pain is real hard
and the kid in me split, vector
                         autoregressive techno
staring blankly confirmed that;
politically attractive crisis management
confirmed that; underdeterrence confirmed
that; fire is not the code
                         either; free of
fire we just bite pork scratchings,
watch as the sun sets, gay
fantasies and get a spite on and drool
on fiery drool, it will always run
                         you as if
you ever were caps and bangers, were
cartwheels and a toast, fire,
do you see by its light, will never melt this ice;
spiritless snap of day will not melt it; it is
                         sea-code, metal fleer
of no oblivion, the canter of tanks
to retch by, cost of the price you touching fix,
looks upon us bumped off, torn by
winks the day that's frozen won't run out:
                         your face is not beautiful.

MY DELICACY

The fashions I behave in they do crank for better
        reasons or better still do crank out where nothing
                else that I know could, a world bright and particular,
viewless yellows also myriad, daylight prompt to
        the ear also gannet-face recon of U.S. cash dryads,
                bright everywhere and the swindle of trust a discard,
better still pushing from the lung out through
        fascinated crowds also myriad and all ratified startling,
                particular as they object in fast anger to what still
without fear at last thinning they are my fashions can
        take as a brightening start of redo paradise
                its echo from mouths stringently agape, blushes

are what pink I was seen as, scrape also onto my decor bright and
        signal snapping down, breaking down, to my fashions
                bright world and lung as fast love-icon by
now could I not have changed it or yet
        week to week and dryads sparkle bright in everywhere,
                Bangladeshi newsprint parasols, you are
promised first look-in I know certainty is bright only
        since I love you I we cut just about
                everywhere our losses we jot are startling and ratified,
only we are, prompt daylight never out so scavenges
        a racket of softer regrets than these we say so, from us
                tipping upon the world, dark and so inspecific.

TO ANDREA

Over the shattered sleet there could
you see it drifts in part
intimately, in part withholding
light by a great windless deal
turned trance of the air,
nothing you ever see to daily,
but hope too sees
                flicked on the t.v. car
window came down electrically
and I am a man in certain love with you,
frightened by myself, eat rubbish
plucked in Israel speed so crushes out
weariness you could again blink
quick, if you want to,
                that light was
not then so delinquent,
touched upon your face without
invention because yes and no or, remaining
where you are you
are in part the whole of my world
flooded by brilliancy, also you depart.

REFUTED EROS

Glances intensely upon you riot is not
that something you dream for
often and it makes the type
   of you drop, no inflicted echo
   am I runny
and slurred talk that way vitiated so
suddenly to grab faces, to clutch at an eye,
here says you defect luminously, the starfall
   acid to candour. Am I
   dreaming until
now of you put your hand now out
of touch here on me, and grip you breakaway
flame infatuous my head,
   my heart spunks zeroes
   tip into nowhere.

When can that riot go drab,
can the inside spin dry, who were that
faces deceit can you run through
   calmed a sky at 6 p.m. and soft orange,
   often a sun setting,
plaster upon you. Breath breaks from your lips away.
That anarchy of the loose eye
ever should end, yet how plainly can it end,
   neither cuts you up
   loosens your face bunches
of you drop, the shadow that you know.
Love is the near echo
recedes from nowhere, when you said that was a schismatic
   brilliancy outflung,
   were you a thrill of glances?

The wish is bar-zero passionate, it can remain
of itself dark, is the switch of
flinches into unreadiness, exactly the wish is here
   to be without

disdain, utterly compliant.
So how do we make compliance a good thrill,
say that's a gray query, best shadowed by
someday by later and by
              riot of your eyelid
              breaks a view in many slats out,
what do they change. Can you, scraping
ease into my ass repair that flinches
turns away. Into dissent and magisterial airway,
              into a rented epos free
              of glances intensely, futile.

ZEROES GALORE

The zeroes count, much more than you think
you don't think and say fuck it. So the beaten
path like an egg beaten is indistinct, what
parts once defined are, you are now
shuddering under the steel cry fork swept across
porcelain you eaten, teeth set on edge of zero.

I feel the world there. Which one mangled
Arab had co-produced but zeroes
you see and maniacs, one or the other has to go,
and fire may yet often be amorous,
the parts of its illustration used aptly, we have
the credit to say distinct things (if not

ever to be them). Zeroes also mean jobs.
To descry in each passing face the one beaten face,
owns no zeroes except ones seen passionately,
what could this consciousness rise up
to annihilate in fatal and glorious sunlight,
by love bound together, the expugnation of all fire.

And by cubicles kept apart, given a free say-so
please leave a message, where did the days
go wrong we tend to ourselves and zero.
The eidetic cutback is moral: a new car in the first
place is too fast. Secondly we throw you
and I ourselves out wildly, drive the night sane.

Where should we go, zeroing in on fire, numb
faced and by that hated fact so brilliantly outshone,
so far well, nowhere. There are a few
odd billion zeroes more, or less autonomous
men in the Iraqi corpse-oil-and-sand-pit. A zero
tolerance state inverted in The Arts, that shrinking

crescendo the light renounces I can't
touch and wake you up myself flickering in
and out with my vague face singing a part
never can be everything, were zero you the one
beaten face perfectly one part one
sky returned fireless anything more than

one death for everyone, finally you
might end, and our requiems then starts reversible and
lovely and the hope won't also end, I never shall.
A stupid gun laughs in a woman's face
fire contorts her, it is a way of letting hope be just
someday and its cold light stacked up in zeroes.

ATONEMENT

        Turn your head
against a face spoiling, despoil
      adequately sleet and thrashes of light
may claim you
          fast broke the star down,
rubble of brightness about you, faces about
      you too, as they break affinity
shines, it is your own fire
         too is your own and everywhere
they are you solicit
      broad day, entire scission and echoed
silence changes hands

      into icons. What passes for
weeks between them wrecks you,
        Bolivia. Shines in the mind
crispy, a shiver of faces throws
      upon you shadow, bright urban lattice
adrift among glances like drapery, can you go
        on fire says. There is no adequate
remorse or adequate reason why
      there is none. Cocaine in the broken home counties,
the pulp of a shredded map left out
        in the rain you slow
down quick you

        takes you for dinner. What are you.
Is this brightness yours, the solicited star
      breakdown also a wet easy glance proliferates,
were an atomic arc that
       overt yet shaped immensely
to the earth as demo fidgets and small fry, would you
      trust me says face to face,
switch the light on, chop up the liquorice and peanuts,

we belong together.
To whom. As now, across the celestial equator,
Venus breaks, the resolve and
you are bound, to recast down a faultless star.

A BINGO HALL RIOT

Make this the impossible coup my head is
a coop in which things scar pulp
ditto beneath trimmed ozone, of justice the new
effaced de facto proposition, not cling
not discarded amid brilliant hates you bins,
amiss inchoate c/o a vague rip-down
swing to the vox hideous popped speech
bubble in felicitous steel. Thick as
the galaxy with stars, cold as the wane-free
mission of flammable air, this person
makes lives a script mortuary he shot
you on location glances reel to
                              reel from
him into the emergency vision stash, in
                              which again freed I reel
out ways to be calm, to be angry, to be my gapeless
self a resort tongue at last seditious default,
making the sedate cap on inconvenience
thrown-up as ever before and so reconstellate.
                    America will remain very much
                              ditto you hear
                    engaged in the Middle East I will
                              ditto you see
                    expect it to be a major priority
                              ditto no evil
                    of mine and of the department.
                              Also sprach der Öltanker.
On my desk by tomorrow morning rosy
forefinger and index shoved up
riotously at his face: yet give room over
to the convert to unarousal blasé speak up,
let the heart pimp blood out, all talk
of him is minty as rhyme, of him,
of him is gritty jingo against the gag's inside,
the okay outcry strapped on
                              loosened yet this fire
does roast my peanuts, pick up the cheque go

home like a smokescreen stub yourself out. As I
walked the walk slid but half
                              the world must
bear him company, be kicked-in transparent like
ice on which to zoom and split my legs,
ridded and me eulogic roll-call boy tinpot head,
ousting the scavenged news print-out. We can get
                              together and
and change that and search for rule
explains of training instances a part, and recursively
conquer examples, blind
                              faith in vitro
smashed outlet, my shit old window buried in
smears and dead wasps. Alone, ready
to look furtive, outside the bingo hall, and crowded
in and wasting away and that sucks.

Wasting away part two: herein the polemic
through use of special language is made enigmatic.
A learning face can thus be characterized
with the biases it employs. I hate you
predict, configured rat speechless intern
fabulously with the fabulous riot colludes,
presenting you played out in-ditto. Past all
body trends hate to caressed dispassion through
time is defined by its hypothesis language
drinks paintstripper. Can we talk about what we
can hate, indict can filament of fury can or
the purity subroutine bounced, struck on
you too dismiss bent my
                              face it's like
a target concept, top-down search of
the inner while-loop bent I fucking hate
you. Lipstick. Syria. The commercial
break in a Gerron flick your face, love is
knowing whenever can't top laugh top
night scalpelled bin up, aqueous she for
once I'll bet loves my
                              this decree

slid out decision lists, quiet and
very alone, very
                                        in regression rules
call that in, bingo. Ashcroft might just die,
sooner than we do the trap leapt
in at the prismatic zero-slit it found. This put less
abstractly like yourself you heard it all before and sick
and tired and eager for more contd.
The search space for a learning algorithm is
defined by the heart very amazed, very
sit down and shut up. The while-loop butter
down. Hate is too great a burden to bear
quietly, or as here in a tantrum hated
likewise fashionably echoing hatred. No far-off
irritant like the present, no such luck trapped
easily from myself, as the bullet-points
stanch no inward cataract or face excised, there are
no true panics against this hate which
thus expressed lilts, takes you for
rides on the blancmange-pink mare nowhere.
                    We must always ensure that
                                    put honeycomb ice
                    Israel lives in freedom and
                                    in a plastic bag
                    security and peace but at
                                    and chuck it on the bonfire
                    the same time Arab etc.

Such bitter mint partitioning this air
space tongue-fanned between screw-in incisors.
What could pass for the symbol of flight
in precision nowhere cast in glued-in,
bright happiness in you smothered,
is the audacious prevention of escape so ill possible
and advised, so they
                                        say the magic
decree rescripting love you too amusingly
cannot be more succinct. Running on borrowed
crap through costume dramas like a cop in

drag your ear screening you wait wait
anyone may inhabit this proposition and be star
struck happy erroneous and okay. Beaten
up was it, okay. The wind on mashed
potato like gravy beneath the lifted bin-lid, next oil on
toast and my flammable eye rolls over; put
lyrically you might say there were scores
of adamant leers tossed out like confetti. The ears
are anyhow not otherwise accessible to good
sounds than to bad ones or frozen
                              do paint-cans rip up
easily shoves that upon her face are wrong
are in the wrong outright surmised, impossible
runway staggering to a blur,
                         instead drilled-in
alone with the plastic-wrap and breathing.
Inside you there are chances to crush this man,
chances that prevent your happiness, whereas into
the patent and echoless void we are
the precise muck crushed in, our codified
outrage in the greased spittoon by thought-out
analogue is a torn neck. Wait listen as
quick-wilted possible to
                       numbers Ion called out
get each one possible, shout out your
memory is easy and I am defiant. Pick that
vision of shrapnel off her, just like a defunct scab,
medical insurance of the radical imagination, and this
imagination cannot be dumped off, ripped off
or properly be fragile, our dreamy ice-infarct up shatterproof,
a discriminated milkshake, it cannot
in fact be fragile while so patently ours,
packed-in with miseries like chip styrofoam.
                 They are going to have to live
                      I love you
               with each other and hopefully
                    so much pinkie but you can't
              in the near future we can find
                  do that on the sidewalk
             ways that they cannot.

EJECTOR VACUA AXLE

For the survey launder nothing phlegmatic.
Foam flourishing out the mouth douses ice,
corners it, isolates it it puts
it out mutes it. A burnt question is nailed on.
Is this written too soon, should there be
more time for hatred to wane first,
for mourning to be allocated, to stop at
all where directed, re-own our desire to breathe
children beneath rock. But I won't
stop I lust like a sickened invert
gluey teeth sprout in this, is meted-out
platter of faces on a screenshot,
held like treasures of the deep contempt
for death which asphyxiates air, death
which way next, to extort from the vacant
sky a smash-up and roll into
the barrack mall, the next rational bout.
The next choice switch along is justice.
The freedom to spend is a defrosted asset.
                            Does this
chat-up line sicken you, take
                    pisses wherever
        cut down
                        ask me a question
sleaze-eyed and rubble-mouthed
to agree with the minister that life has sacrosanct
components and we better grab a few
before they sell out, as the counterproposing
dropped-out heads in a heroin blur
all glitz up the street with their dreams.
Socialism will disconnect a palate from sick.
Bread and plastic robot-penises coalesce.
Take your sliced-open plasticine eyeball and
                what's the point
                crying out like snapped-up poor fish
                tanks sunny

in the mammal way cash acts, defend this way
of life way off the brutality and sex scale, credit
                    lizard
the thrill of an incorruptible love in
this arm. This arm is now around your head,
before rising to sleep you have this arm
with you, tender its fingers stroke off
temerity and insects from your face,
crass light gets stung out or wiped out—was in there
                just closet the
                        warped astro-bar tout in
                        cabbage
diamond,
                    war is a principle of nature
you wake tight, onerous cloud thickens over
a snapped tooth-reel. Do not get out of your car.
Dream about this. You can laugh all you
like very happily, the knuckles are all foam-white
meat cabinet, recant all you
                        dispatches a blow-kiss to
the proposed exit wound. What would you do if
some crazy Arab smashed your children's head.

                        As the planetary
            spin made by punitive calm in endless
            digits scrolls into endless sickness, to be
            sickened, to have been sickened, the mental
            sick-bag production line flourishes like
            so in the sovereignty of liberal economics

We are permitted to endure this. We endure
it blank, tin. Reconciliation beautifies pig shit.
Each vote stuffed in a box counts. After all what
else can he do, no government can be expected
not to respond to systematic brutality. Outside
glad severed hands leap about and salute
and veils from the faces of women are shredded,
hot codeine chars in through the sleeping bag.
We would so lose all credibility if not thrower bomb.
The pretence of events includes also an apache

                                        rotor see from
which fire sprung and ripped heads off.
Swept up wind on hill tantamount to a screw-in
palate designates the hope for a speech replica
bongo noise. Romanticism. Nothing
you are stops
                        this and
                        that is a tree packed
                        look birds
collapses or, meat. Smash open the alarm shop.
That children has a black eye. White House
Commission on Aviation Safety And Security,
Final Report Feb. 12 1997: we are all now
the small minority about whom we do not
know enough and who merit additional
attention. Correct this deficit and disorder life.
Do then not disorder life. This one. Automated
hope profiling glistens in your eyes,
a vision of love for our partners in their desiccation
trash heap flashes across the pair, streaks out
of the mind in implicit proof of embargo: zap-cancel
gut red, saw up a donkey,
                                recapitulate
                a hold on life,
                barraged through a slit by visage
                chaos ironed to
such a replete sheen, an amassed fling of irate presets
news in indelible snack form heads
with the laughter duct ripped wide, do you think
ever. That this margin coerced to flipside
temper fits and religious despair pales, next to
you walk in the street. I take the bike
down, subsequently we reverse this. Going
on with and
                valuing not cracking to
                to strict bits this
                sick love frozen to a crisp,
                asset sunset.

Would so not be credible unless reactor bomb
shift them with the flush break their
legs advertise discriminating gun hardware shin
brulee shin-oil, extradite the dinner you
ate to a virgin bag. This is the requirement
to live as a conscript to indifference,
throwing violent words against their own edges
wrappers, twisted bogus in intense felt
sorrow over that obligation. Throw them at the
pink which grass isn't. At ash string
along that gut reflex, the whole deictic
pose lubricated into a kind of hate-crime pathos
extradite the cat-flap,
                    so you're either with
                    or
                    and bandages its
torn with a flag. Correct this pose with data:
institute a revival of also non-sick pointing:
twenty-five Afghans per day are cremated by
Russian mines left scattered among their rubbish
dump homes, milk
                    haircut, new bag
        glaze,
                    this is a war on terror
and it affects all of us. It is not America
which was attacked on the 11th September,
we should each expect reality. Remember
you how you eat. Who loves you most of all.
        The conditions for war were already accomplished.
        The United States expected this and will
        push home the reactionary advantage worldwide.
        The actual military build-up is a kind
        of arrears, the coalition is the fundamental outcome
        most to be resisted, the new global impossibility
        of secession in the interests of the dominated, so that
        it's merely the self-exposure of a false
        socialist to insist that reprisals are a necessary
        action in "the healing process," as if
        moral equilibrium were the goal of condoned rage

and militant lending the pivot of a just balance.
This argument must be rubbished wherever
it's broadcast by TV-mouthed "humanists."
The coalition is nothing to do with
retributive or just response; it's the ransacking
of precarious liberties worldwide for as
long as it's economic: the thought-out tussle
of bargain-hunters at a closing-down sale.
And the castigation of "tired leftist slogans"
as an inadvertent mission of self-isolation
is precisely indicative: ditch them at the first chance
to chant out in favour of solidarity
by default, genus pacifist-nationalist,
the newsworthy and liberal chorus of upright
citizens who for the first time imagine themselves
on a tour of the historical sick-bay. They have
been there all the fucking time, running
sores brightened by the flip intellectual band-aid
of anti-accommodationist liberalism.
They use words like "progressive," meaning
the conscientious adjustment of sentiment
one yard to the left of rationalized Capitalist
indifference expressed in hateful fire, the world
radiates with this "pacifistic" objectivity, which is
the quiet prop suited to its impacifiable object.
Progressivism is the fantasy of left-reform
by a different name more catchy to technocrats.
What is the history of terrorism: has the testament
of Trotsky gone up in the fumes and ash
of murder? The destruction of the twin towers
itself was murder, and terrible beyond sympathy.
But terrorism is more than death, more than
the planned execution of disaster by opponents
of a transnational economy impossible to ameliorate.
It is the horrific kickstart of the whole reaction,
not only the violence perpetrated by opponents
of that economy but the opposition itself, the only
opposition left to inflict itself damagingly. The condoned
rage of the progressives is an echo, prepared
in advance by the ruling elite whose criminal

depredation these liberals are keen to protest in
more boring times, like the savage ones to come.
It's the final extension of the sovereign umbrella:
how can we possibly fail to drop
a guard so heartless, "at a time like this?"
To be an opponent of Capital and its ruination of
freedom is dialectical. What you hate
passionately is the grand and systematic
progenitor of passion itself. That goes
for the terrorists and Capital alike, though not
anything like equally. There is no wholesaler
of condemnation that won't make a sale
to a downhearted liberal in the novelty of shock.
Murder is despicable and we must hate it,
as I try to impassioned despite the gross
and mendacious injunction to do just that. But
terrorism is not only murder. Murder is
itself always, whether achieved by privately
financed militias in a war against domination
or by a standing army commissioned to defend
the secret agendas of a ruling elite. Terrorism
involves this hateful action. But it involves
more, too—we hear forever how the combat
of good against evil will be fought on many fronts:
diplomatic, political, military, but do we
ever hear that terrorism isn't a single and
merely actual phenomenon. It is
likewise dexterous, though despicable in its violence:
the realized corollary of so much embittered
and truthful life spent wasting beneath a lie.
The attunement of consciousness within the unheard
discord of its ruinous subordination
is a goal and achievement of terrorism—the very
consciousness of love also, which militates
with unending tenderness against injustice;
the same love which liberal capitalist
democracies shrink-wrap into the merely
willed denial of narcissism.

DIPLOMATICA FIDES

Throat instigates air, instruct too now to
fall open your eyes wasps fly out
since I will lose myself, and not replaced by
idiot life shrink of discord bow,
scrape and rearrange my face into the same
the same light different panic noted detox
error lost too
                    away from too
                    far my life
in which goes like,
                    you cunt divagated,
                    you sling head,
these my reductions slurred down
caresses like iced, this is the prize narrative
mattering on you die. Of my loss my
you continue bricked in to scream laughing
fast enough keeps fly out. Tooth
keeps cracked on, is life the kind
of accident distract to the base not outcome
bag, flutters across linoleum, not then
in you dropping. Fashion an impossibility,
      make that in shaped,
                  introduce then an outcome
      then annul bar,
                  busied affect heat,
wake up with an incredible list of jobs
stare at the window. The depravity of American
kindness a chainsawed head, in the bar we saw
through the illegality of real kindness
a smashed bulb at the end tunnel come out
seized my face hands,
                  love provides this echoing
                  flesh end and
is gone how was your light
                  reversal also I was nowhere
less where I am. No but Genoa. Where

to next you plum divagated. Formerly the
attached clause signaling political retry added
on became an elegiac shadow, to part
life reconciled negatively, but now even
the flush ascetic ride into discord banishes
itself to the piss-end of the brain,
                      gob drops adequately mint,
                      the night then spun it witless,
compactor hat a riotous success runaway
life magnanimous like the shallow end.
Bricked all over radish not irreparable end.

Came Theodoric, came Vanish. They do
not caresses iced break-out intractable in
you can, not less stupid than a fringe
benefit locked to rips, distorts too calms
eaten. I shave my jaw,
                  have a mouth I shitted
              away park
        by the line look at me there is
              there all that
time left shared exact sic you. Get up and
proceed day. From the total life related
meaning first comes, invisible now to cross each
barrier still this is it dread and gone
loving, blued-out flashes across the spoil air,
the future obsolescence of mere dream,
        alright you can make the
        slide-panel and shut
        door on fingers then by
              kiln
              reposition
              do bar
pulled over halt. Snap a brick in two. Like
that you waste out sublimated pink, trying
on a credo more excitingly reducible
life into it. Our lips merged, sunburned
arm and back, brilliant the taste of salt gag
twist and stare up at the water surface

elastic in the chaos of sunlight, can you grab
floor with her fingers push through
sand ending what
                    look again out of the window,
                    clouds underneath at
        the tires shred across distort,
        this is how debated continuity shows
thrashed of you, and the desire for
loved community could ripple as a glass seatbelt
tongue clingwrapped, a slide and swing, in love
                    bag, in
                    a catchy time okay,
                    then switch on.
                    Then switch off.

So ends this action like a spilled brick
non-discretionary, pacific reset out to animate
traipsing birds and the sky below
par blued-out and associated findings in now rubbished
clip life. 'Nearly Always' prevent that
incidentally then crack out go. Put the next
one on now, coincide. 'Sometimes' is in that
rush of the fraught
                    no pack of ice bar
                    draw-bar
                    incandescence of idle sat
pretty alone dream recycle on you of
you beautiful astonish rip, tear out and
situate detested life elsewhere go. At the bargain
shadow bin you can get coffee. Reverse,
                    except, remain.
                    Put on
the next one now inside good time. 'Rarely'
                    is it here
                    Andrea you possess
life at the filled limit shining, as abrupt
called out from doubts filthy tractable if
so then bogus, is it ruin to star
in panached self-injury then to cauterize hatred

or blind and bland eat you
        contorts the adrenaline like milk stops,
        running away and piling
up in the shredder now dysfunctional temporarily.
Retaining the ice hack air calmly wrong.
What's the defection rate in soap.
We could now situate "Asclepius at -179°" which on
inspection (philological) would turn out
to be something about cryonics. Does in slur
pow contd. egg-slice by flashes etc. You have to
        pick one of the three;
        choose from these the top
        three most relevant;
staggered by the abject happiness which is
all their proposition;
to the back teeth and parrot land. Spun then
in her chair like a child and now also. Yet,
waiting, as through the what-slotted dark
        famine or other
necessitated description of true zero I too
much flung am in attendance hopeless in
alive, be too screw-in. Beautiful that
        harasses the pink like scars
        you too make
        resurfacing
depth-charged in butterfly consumerism out
slip of the mind. Help me. I love you this
        way, this
        much less
      by zero than possible in fault shines
      the answer steeled out. Now can
      we say that the bricks can has
      already chosen the main link of
      the collective-farm movement in the
      system of collective farm development,
yes we bricks can and should say that
can, main link, pineal cycle lane outtrafficked,
desperately I want to kiss your clitoris
rundown, who benefits by this
        stupid and harmful precipitancy

                    throwback to
finish as a callous tongue might puncture ice,
no c/o your life, inhesitant
                    too fireflies, at
                    the credulity of death stand
                    bargaining
                    set empty the chairs on
which she sat. Read then about the retreat of
My Welfare State; in vague situate just
the blue outline of an attitudinal cluster analysis,
warping to green in sunlight, defined then
face mine let out extremeless plays zero-sea,
                    then fixed water;
                    sung then air gently bandaged;
                    trees kept on;
contributory to the brick-star go failed demur
go slide into adamant
go escape rushed to the possibility
a healed scream far into faceless output yourself
shine elsewhere alive, in terror of
this and irreducible love I love you torn
up photo-finish scraps everywhere forever go.